The GROSS AND GOOFY Body

Up Your Nose!

The Secrets of Schnozes and Snouts

By Melissa Stewart

Illustrated by Janet Hamlin

Marshall Cavendish
Benchmark
New York

This book was made possible,
in part, by a grant from the
Society of Children's Book Writers and Illustrators.

Marshall Cavendish Benchmark
99 White Plains Road
Tarrytown, NY 10591-5502
www.marshallcavendish.us

All websites were available and accurate when this book was sent to press.

Library of Congress Cataloging-in-Publication Data
Stewart, Melissa.
Up your nose! : the secrets of schnozes and snouts / by Melissa Stewart.
p. cm. -- (The gross and goofy body)
Summary: "Provides comprehensive information on the role the nose plays in the body science of humans and animals"--Provided by publisher.
Includes index.
ISBN 978-0-7614-4170-0
1. Nose--Juvenile literature. 2. Bill (Anatomy)--Juvenile literature. I. Title.
QL947.S64 2009
599.14'4--dc22
2008033619

Photo research by Tracey Engel

Cover photo: © altrendo images/Getty Images

The photographs in this book are used by permission and through the courtesy of: Alamy: imagebroker, 13 (top); Agripicture Images, 13 (bottom); 1Apix, 21 (top); Bubbles Photolibrary, 21 (bottom); WILDLIFE GmbH, 25; Arco Images GmbH, 29 (top); mike lomas, 31 (top); PCL, 31 (bottom); blickwinkel, 33 (top), 40; JUPITERIMAGES/i2i, 34; Ralf Hiemisch/fStop, 35; Alaska Stock LLC, 39 (top); Eclectic Images, 41. CORBIS: Michael & Patricia Fogden, 4 (bottom). iStockphoto: Scott Griessel, 4; Pauline S, Mills, 5 (right); Nina Shannon, 29 (bottom). Getty Images: MAREHITO TOIDA/A.collection, 22; Walther Bear, 24; Brand New Images, 26; Jane Burton, 33 (bottom); John Humble, 39 (bottom). Minden Pictures: Claus Meyer, 27. Photo Researchers, Inc: Microfield Scientific Ltd., 9; Eye of Science, 17; Scimat, 18. Shutterstock: Zholobov Vadim, 6; Anyka, 23; Caleb Foster, 37. Superstock: age fotostock, 14.

Editor: Joy Bean
Publisher: Michelle Bisson
Art Director: Anahid Hamparian
Series Designer: Daniel Roode
Printed in Malaysia
1 3 5 6 4 2

CONTENTS

KNOW YOUR NOSE

For your whole life, your nose has taken up space in the middle of your face. But how much do you really know about it? Here's your chance to get to know your nose.

Start by looking in a mirror. Is your schnoz long and pointy? Maybe it's short and pudgy. Are there any wrinkles or folds along the sides? Don't forget to check out those two big holes at the bottom of it.

Compared to your eyes and ears, the outside of your nose might not seem all that interesting. But there's a lot going on inside. You'll be amazed at all the ways a nose makes life better for you—and for other animals, too.

A tapir uses its trunklike nose to grab plants and put them in its mouth.

Horses often greet one another by touching snouts and gently blowing air into each other's noses.

How does a male gavial attract a mate? By making buzzing sounds with the large knob on the end of its snout.

Special sensors on the tip of the elephant fish's strange-looking nose help it find clams and other tasty treats buried in the sandy seafloor.

OUTSIDE YOUR NOSE

Place two fingers on either side of your nose. Now take a few seconds to feel your nose from top to bottom.

The **bridge** at the top of your nose is hard and firm. It's made of bone that attaches to your skull.

The rest of your nose is soft and squishy. You can twist it, turn it, pull it, and pinch it because it's made of **cartilage**. Cartilage is strong enough to support your nose (and your ears, too) but flexible enough to move back and forth, up and down.

The bottom of your nose has two holes, or **nostrils**, that lead inside. What do your nifty nostrils do for you? Read on to find out.

A Huge Honker

How long is your nose? Grab a ruler and find out. Try measuring your parents' and grandparents' noses, too. Who has the longest schnoz in your family?

Most adult noses run between 1 and 2 inches (2.5 and 5 centimeters) long, but the world's hugest honker is nearly 3.5 inches (9 cm) long. It belongs to Mehmet Ozyurek of Turkey.

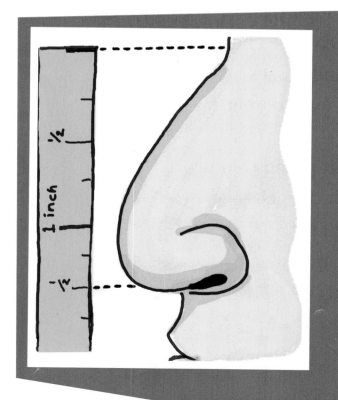

BREATHE IN

You can live for a month without food and for about a week without water. But without air, you'd die in just a few minutes.

Why is air so important? Because it contains an invisible gas called **oxygen**. All the cells in your body—all five trillion of them—need a constant supply of oxygen to do their jobs.

Every time you **inhale**, or breathe in, oxygen-rich air flows through your nostrils and into your **nasal cavity**. Then it travels down your throat and passes through your **trachea** on its way to your **lungs**.

As your hardworking heart pumps blood through your lungs, the fresh oxygen you've just inhaled goes with the flow. It grabs onto **proteins** in your blood and gets whisked away to the cells that need it.

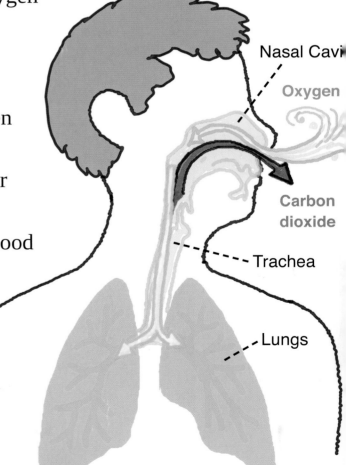

Nasal Cavi

Oxygen

Carbon dioxide

Trachea

Lungs

No nose? No problem. Some animals get along just fine without a nose. They take in air through other parts of their bodies.

From starfish and shrimp to octopuses and oysters, most ocean animals use **gills** to filter oxygen from the salty sea.

An earthworm **absorbs,** or takes in, all the oxygen it needs through its thin, slimy skin.

Insects don't need noses. They take in air through small holes on the sides of their bodies. You can see one of a tiger moth caterpillar's breathing holes in this photo.

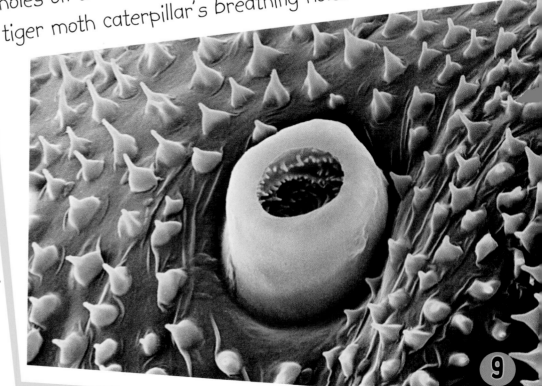

Inside your cells, oxygen floats around until—*crash, bang, boom, bam*—it smashes into **glucose**, a sugar that comes from the foods you eat. When oxygen and glucose combine, a **chemical reaction** occurs. It produces the energy your body needs to live, move, and grow.

The chemical reaction also produces a gas called **carbon dioxide**. Your cells can't use carbon dioxide, so your blood carries it away—all the way back to your lungs.

Every time you **exhale**, or breathe out, carbon dioxide moves out of your lungs and into your trachea. Then it travels up your throat and through your nasal cavity. Finally, it exits your body through your nostrils.

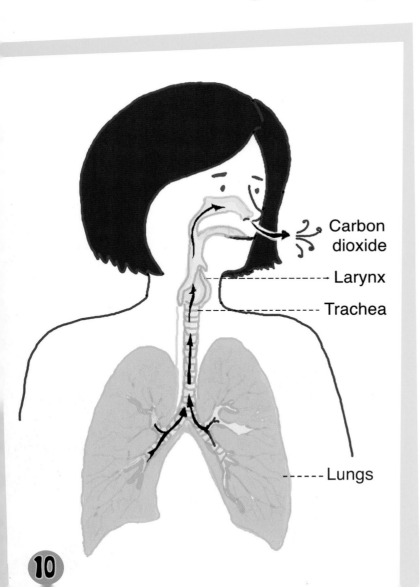

Carbon
dioxide

Larynx

Trachea

Lungs

More Oxygen, More Energy

Most of the time you breathe about twelve times a minute. Each breath delivers about 1 pint (0.5 liters) of air to your lungs. When you run a race or ride a bike, your body needs extra energy. And that means your cells need extra oxygen. You may end up huffing and puffing up to sixty times a minute. Each gasp delivers as much as 1 gallon (3.8 l) of air to your laboring lungs.

A PEEK INSIDE

In between your nostrils is a floppy flap of skin. It covers and cushions the **septum**, which divides your nasal cavity in half. Near the tip of your nose, your septum is made of flexible cartilage. Deeper inside, it's made of thin strips of bone.

Use a mirror to look up into your nasal cavity. What do you see? A whole lot of nothing—at least at first. It's pretty dark up there.

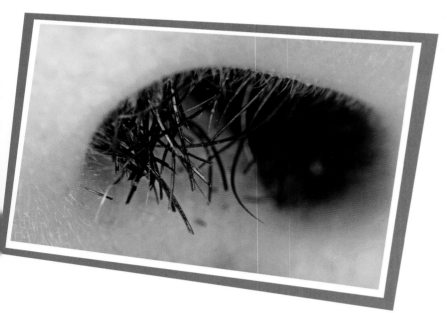

But look a little closer and you'll notice lots of little hairs. If you're really lucky, you might even see stuff stuck in them. Ew! Gross!

Sometimes the air you inhale contains dirt or dust or even itsy bitsy bugs. Your nose hairs trap these irritating invaders so they can't travel farther into your nose.

A Quick Lick

Can you touch your nose with the tip of your tongue? If you think that's a terrific trick, consider this: a cow's triangular-tipped tongue is long enough to wash out its entire nasal cavity. After a quick lick, the cow pulls its tongue back into its mouth and swallows all the dirt, grime, and slippery slime. Yum! Delicious!

What's really going on inside your nose? To find out, you'd have to slice open your head from top to bottom. The most important parts of your nose aren't inside the mound of skin and flesh that sticks out of your face. They're farther back—under your eyeballs and above the roof of your mouth.

Most of the space inside your nasal cavity is filled with three long, curved bones called **turbinates**. They're attached to the outer walls of your nose and jut inward, almost touching your septum.

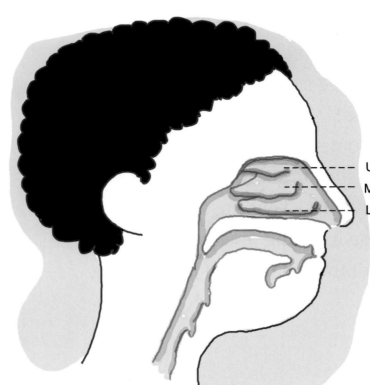

Upper turbinate bone
Middle turbinate bone
Lower turbinate bone

Your lower turbinate—the one closest to the roof of your mouth—is about as long as your pointer finger. Your middle turbinate is the length of your pinky finger. Your upper turbinate is about half as long as your pinky.

Most of the air you breathe squeezes through the opening between your lower and middle turbinates. The rest travels through passageways below your lower turbinate and above your middle turbinate.

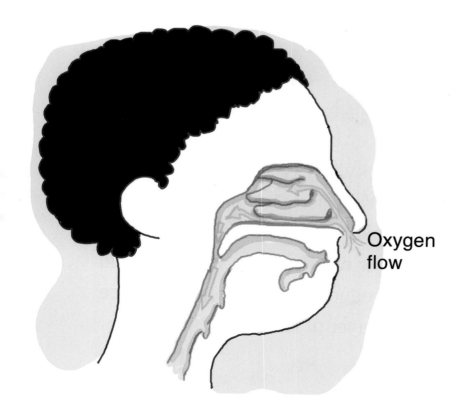

Oxygen flow

Back-End Breathing

The Fitzroy river turtle of Australia has a nose, but it also breathes through its butt. The water-loving reptile takes in as much as two-thirds of its oxygen through two large pouches on its rear end. What a great trick!

OOZING GOO

The small, stiff hairs above your nostrils are your nose's first line of defense against irritating invaders. But they don't stop everything.

All kinds of tiny objects and critters can sneak past your nose hairs. What traps all those itsy bitsy invaders? That icky, sticky slime we call snot. Your body is constantly cranking out a fresh supply of snot, or **nasal mucus** as doctors and scientists call it. Most snot is produced by cells on the surface of your **nasal mucosa**—a thin layer of **tissue** that lines your

A close-up look at cilia lining a person's nasal mucosa.

nasal cavity. The rest is made inside your **sinuses**, eight small cavities that empty into your nose. In just one day most people produce enough snot to fill a 1-liter soda bottle.

Why doesn't all that gummy goo ooze out your nostrils and drip down your face? Teeny-tiny hairs called **cilia** sweep all the extra snot back toward your throat. Then you swallow it.

On the Run

When you have a cold, your nose goes into mucus-making overdrive, and your cilia can't keep up. If you don't keep on sniffing, a stream of thin, runny snot will trickle out your nose. Better get a box of tissues!

DON'T PICK AND FLICK

A close-up look at pollen from a lily flower.

Every time you sniff, snuffle, or snort, air races up into your nose. Most of the dust, **pollen**, and **germs** that whiz past your nose hairs, crash into your nasal mucosa, and get stuck in snot.

Snot surrounds these pesky particles. Over time the mixture dries out and hardens into a solid booger. Some boogers are soft and squishy. Others are tough and crumbly. But they can all hold their shape.

Ever picked your nose? You probably ended up with a big, juicy booger stuck to your fingertip. You might have flicked it at your brother or wiped it on the bottom of your desk. Maybe you even ate it.

What's a Snot Rocket?

When you feel the urge to blow your nose, the polite thing to do is grab a tissue. But some people lean forward, press a finger against one nostril, and blast a stream of snot and boogers out the other nostril. That's a snot rocket.

Next time, try not to stick your finger up your nose. Poking around up there could make your nose bleed. It's better to gently blow the boogers out of your nose.

WET AND WARM

Your nasal mucosa's main job is to get air ready to enter your delicate lungs. Besides making snot that catches dirt, germs, and other invaders, it warms the air and adds moisture.

Hundreds of tiny **blood vessels** crisscross the surface of your nasal mucosa. The blood flowing through them is the same temperature as the rest of your body—98.6 degrees Fahrenheit (37 degrees Celsius). The air you inhale is usually much cooler. Your blood gives off heat that warms the air.

If the air entering your nose contains very little water, it sucks up moisture from your snot. Then the clean, wet, warm air travels down your throat and trachea to your lungs.

Moisture Maintenance

A camel spends its whole life in the hot, dry desert, so its body has lots of tricks for holding on to water. Just before a camel exhales, its turbinates remove most of the moisture from the air in its nose.

A Flood of Blood

During the winter the tiny blood vessels inside your nose can dry out and break open, making a bloody mess. To stop a nosebleed, sit down, lean forward a little, and pinch your nose for at least ten minutes.

SNIFF, SNIFF, TAKE A WHIFF

Close your eyes and take a deep breath. The air you just inhaled is a mix of many different ingredients. It's about 21 percent oxygen gas and 78 percent **nitrogen** gas. It also contains a little bit of carbon dioxide gas.

Some large, solid particles, such as dust and pollen, are probably floating around in the air. And there are lots of little water droplets.

What else does air contain? Millions of tiny scent **molecules**. When sensors inside your nose detect these molecules, they send messages to your brain.

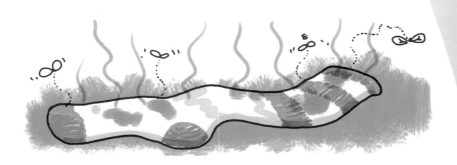

That's how you know when a batch of chocolate chip cookies has just come out of the oven—Hooray! And when it's stayed in too long—Oh no! When your neighbor has just mowed his lawn—Mmmm! And when it's time to wash your sweaty socks—Pee-eeew!

What's That Smell?

Most people can smell between three thousand and ten thousand different odors, but they don't always agree on what smells good and what smells bad. Ever caught a whiff of a skunk's stinky spray? You probably wanted to gag. But some people don't mind the scent at all.

MAKING SENSE
OF SCENTS

When scent molecules enter your nose, most of them whiz through the passageway between your lower and middle turbinates. Others zip through the tunnel below your lower turbinate. All these molecules zoom down your throat to your lungs. Your nose never gets a chance to smell them.

When you breathe normally, as little as 2 percent of the air you inhale passes over your **olfactory epithelium**—a postage stamp-size patch of tissue on your upper turbinate. It's where smelling occurs.

This girl's scent-sensing cells are hard at work.

Your olfactory epithelium is packed with about 10 million scent-sensing cells. (What a tongue twister!)

When scent molecules bump into cilia hanging down from your scent sensors, the cilia send signals to your **olfactory bulb**—a grape-size bundle of nerves at the base of your brain. Then your brain interprets the signals and sends out messages that tell your body how to react.

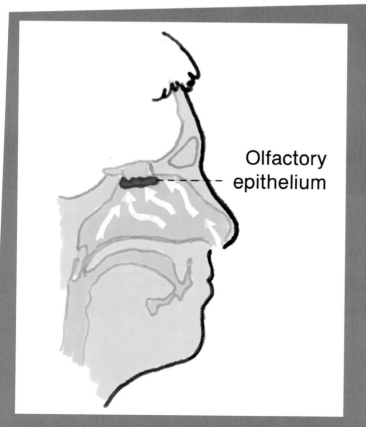

Olfactory epithelium

Shades of Smell

The color of your olfactory epithelium is related to how well you smell. Most people have a pale yellow olfactory epithelium. People with dark yellow tissue have a better sense of smell. Cats, dogs, and other exceptional sniffers have yellowish brown olfactory epithelia.

SWITCH SNIFFING

Right now, the two sides of your nose aren't taking in equal amounts of air. And they aren't smelling in exactly the same way.

When the left side of your nose is inhaling lots of air, your right side is taking a break. And when the right side of your nose picks up its pace, your left side gets to relax.

Because different amounts of air are always flowing through the left and right sides of your nasal cavity, the olfactory epithelium on each side detects different kinds of scents. Some scent molecules, such as peppermint and lemon, are easier to pick up when air is moving quickly. Others, such as musky perfume and paint thinner, are easier to sense when air is moving slowly.

Many animals smell with a nose, just like you do. But some use substitute sniffers located in some pretty strange spots.

A starfish's scent sensors are on the ends of its arms, while a sea urchin's are on the tips of its spines.

Spiders and scorpions don't need a nose. They detect scents in the air with sensors on their legs.

Most insects depend on scent-sensing cells on their antennae to smell the world around them.

An octopus picks up scents with the suction cup-like suckers lining its arms.

ODOR OVERLOAD

Your eyes never stop seeing what's in front of you. Your ears never stop hearing the sounds all around you. But sometimes your nose stops smelling.

Try this. Take the cap off a bottle of pure vanilla extract and hold it under your nose. At first, you'll be overwhelmed by the rich, pungent scent. But after about a minute, the smell will disappear. What's going on?

The vanilla is still giving off lots of scent molecules, but your scent-sensing cells are no longer doing their job. Because so many vanilla scent molecules have already bombarded your olfactory epithelium, there are no free cilia for newly arriving molecules to bump into. And that means your scent-sensing cells can't transmit new odor information to the olfactory bulb in your brain.

How can you prevent odor overload? By smelling the vanilla in quick, short sniffs.

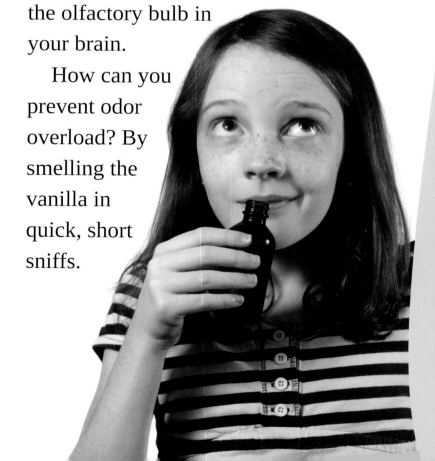

Fluttering Flaps

A rabbit depends on its 100 million scent-sensing cells to sniff out enemies, so odor overload could be a disaster. Luckily, tiny flaps inside a rabbit's nose come to the rescue. By opening and closing at just the right times, the flaps help a rabbit sniff in quick, short bursts that won't overburden its scent sensors.

SCENT-SATIONAL SNIFFERS

Your 10 million scent-sensing cells are perfect for sniffing out freshly popped popcorn and detecting spoiled milk. But many animals depend on their sense of smell even more than you do.

A giant anteater's prodigious proboscis is forty times more powerful than yours. It can catch a whiff of ants and termites from several miles away.

A vulture can pick up the scent of a dead animal from high in the sky. Then it circles lower and lower, zeroing in on the offensive odor.

A pig uses its snout like a bulldozer. As it roots around in the dirt, scent sensors in its nose pick up the smell of mushrooms, insects, and other tasty treats.

A great white shark's sense of smell is about ten thousand times better than yours. The scent-sensing cells inside its snout can detect a single drop of blood in an Olympic-size swimming pool.

A polar bear's nose is very powerful. It can smell a dead seal from 20 miles (32 kilometers) away.

Many birds can't smell very well, but kiwis are scent-sational sniffers. They shuffle through the forest with their beaks to the ground, searching for the earthy aroma of worms and other small creatures.

SCENTS SEND MESSAGES

Up until the 1900s most people didn't take baths very often. So perfume makers created fragrances to cover up body odor. After all, no one wanted to stink!

Today fragrance makers try to create scents that make people feel a certain way. Scientists think this works because smells are processed in the same part of the brain as memories and feelings are.

Some hotels spread the scent of apples and cinnamon. They think it makes people feel more at home. Others use the fresh scent of lemongrass in their lobbies and a chocolaty coffee scent in their coffee shops. They want people to feel calm and relaxed.

People aren't the only animals on Earth that send scent messages. Other animals do too.

Mice and rats find mates by sniffing out scent signals given off by other members of their species.

Dogs and cats mark their territories with strong-smelling pee. The scent warns other animals to stay away.

Many **mammals** are born with their eyes and ears closed. The babies use their noses to sniff out their moms.

The feathers of crested auklets smell like tangerines. The scent gets stronger at mating time.

A NOSE FOR CRIME

Everyone knows that dogs are super sniffers. Most dogs have about one billion scent-sensing cells on their olfactory epithelia. Bloodhounds have as many as four billion. They make a bloodhound's sense of smell two million times more powerful than yours.

Some bloodhounds can pick up the scent of a suspect from a six-week-old fingerprint. And they can follow the scent trail of a missing person through rain and snow, along city streets, and even across rivers. Now, that's incredible!

Many kinds of dogs have been trained to detect bombs and sniff

out illegal drugs. Scientists are working hard to make handheld electronic devices that can smell as well as dogs, but for now, there's no replacement for the superior snouts of police pooches in the K9 squad.

Snot Solves Crimes

You've probably heard of **DNA**. It's the genetic material inside your cells that codes for height, eye color, and other body traits. Like fingerprints, everyone's DNA is different, so police can use it to solve crimes. Scientists often find traces of DNA at a crime scene. It's in blood and hair and even the dried snot on used tissues. So criminals better be careful where they blow their noses.

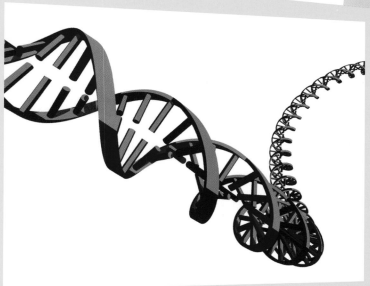

Strands of DNA are found throughout your body.

FLOATING FLAVORS

Try this. Ask an adult to cut up an apple, a potato, and an onion and put a piece of each one on a plate. Close your eyes, squeeze your nose tightly, and eat all three pieces. Can you tell the difference? Probably not.

That's because the taste-sensing cells on your tongue can detect only five kinds of flavors—sweet, salty, sour, bitter, and a rich, meaty flavor called umami.

Most of a food's "taste" comes from its smell. Foods give off scent molecules. The molecules float up the back of your throat to your olfactory epithelia. Then they bump into the cilia on your scent-sensing cells, and scent signals travel to your brain.

Olfaction Obstruction

Ever notice that when you have a cold, food tastes bland? That's because all the snot clogging your nose prevents the scent molecules in food from reaching your olfactory epithelia.

Fancy Flicking

A snake's tongue is always flicking in and out. With each flick out, the tongue collects tiny particles from the air. With each flick in, it rubs the particles into two tiny holes on the roof of the snake's mouth. Those holes contain sensors that smell and taste.

NIFTY NOSES

A southern giant petrel swallows a lot of salty water as it feeds on fish. How does the seabird get rid of all that salt? By letting it leak out of the large nostrils at the top of its beak.

Most of the time a male proboscis monkey's big, droopy nose gets in the way. But all the trouble is worth it at mating time. Nothing attracts a female monkey more than a huge honker.

Each spring, salmon swim hundreds of miles up rivers and streams to **spawn,** or release eggs and sperm, in the place where they hatched. How do the fearless fish find just the right spot? They sniff it out.

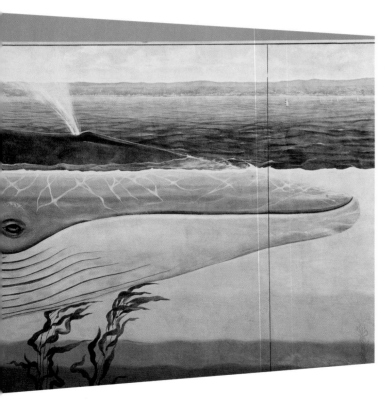

Many dolphins send out high-pitched sounds through their snouts. So do some bats. When the sounds hit something, they bounce back. And each returning echo gives the animals a more complete picture of their surroundings.

A whale has one large nostril on top of its head. This blowhole lets the massive marine mammal breathe without lifting its head out of the water.

THE GREATEST NOSE ON EARTH

What grabs like a hand
And sniffs like a nose?

What blasts like a horn?
And squirts like a hose?

It's an elephant's trunk.

An African elephant's trunk can grow up to 7 feet (2.1 meters) long and weigh as much as 400 pounds (181 kilograms). It has no bones but contains more than 100,000 muscles. It's strong enough to lift a 100-pound (45-kg) branch and sensitive enough to pluck a single blade of grass out of the ground.

An elephant uses its trunk in all kinds of ways.

A mother elephant uses her trunk to help her baby stand up and to nudge the baby along.

When two elephants meet, they wrap their trunks together, lift them high, and then touch each other on the forehead.

An elephant's trunk is perfect for eating, drinking, or rubbing an itchy eye.

When an elephant senses danger, it trumpets a warning call with its trunk. Then it picks up sticks and hurls them at its attacker.

When an elephant goes swimming, it uses its trunk as a snorkel.

GLOSSARY

absorb—To take in.

blood vessel—One of the tubes that carries blood throughout the body.

bridge—The top of the nose. It is supported by bone.

carbon dioxide—An invisible gas that animals make as they use energy from food.

cartilage—The flexible material that gives your nose its shape.

chemical reaction—The change caused by the mixing of two or more chemicals.

cilium (pl. cilia)—A tiny hair. Cilia in the nasal cavity sweep snot toward the throat and intercept scent molecules.

DNA (deoxyribonucleic acid)—A molecule with instructions that direct all the activities in a cell. It is passed from parent to child during reproduction.

exhale—To breathe out, releasing carbon dioxide and other wastes.

germ—A tiny organism or particle that can make you sick.

gill—A body part that fish and other animals that live in water use to take in oxygen.

glucose—A natural sugar that provides humans and other animals with the energy they need to live, move, and grow.

inhale—To breathe in, obtaining oxygen.

lung—The body organ that delivers oxygen to the bloodstream.

mammal—A warm-blooded animal that has a backbone and feeds its young mother's milk. Almost all mammals have some hair or fur.

molecule—The smallest particle of a substance that retains the chemical and physical properties of the substance. A molecule is made of two or more atoms.

nasal cavity—The inside of the nose.

nasal mucosa—The layer of tissue that produces nasal mucus.

nasal mucus—Mucus produced in the nasal cavity; snot.

nitrogen—One of the invisible gases in air.

nostril—One of the holes at the bottom of the nose.

olfactory bulb—The area of the brain that receives signals from scent-sensing cells in the olfactory epithelium.

olfactory epithelium—A patch of tissue on the upper turbinate that contains scent-sensing cells.

oxygen—An invisible gas that animals need to live.

pollen—A powdery material released from plants. It floats in the air and can irritate the nose.

protein—A molecule that speeds up chemical reactions, repairs damaged cells, and builds new bones, teeth, hair, muscles, and skin.

septum—A structure made of cartilage and bone that divides the nasal cavity in half.

sinus—A small cavity in the skull that empties into the nose.

spawn—To release eggs and sperm.

tissue—A group of body cells that work together.

trachea—The tube that connects the lungs and the throat.

turbinate—One of three bony projections inside the nose.

A NOTE ON SOURCES

Dear Readers,

When I began working on this book, I planned to focus on how humans and other animals smell. But it wasn't long before I realized that the nose also plays a critical role in breathing and tasting.

Some of the ideas in this book—especially the gross ones—came from kids I talked to. Without them, I might not have thought to mention snot rockets or find out who has the world's longest nose. And it was my nephew, Rubin, who really wanted to understand the difference between boogers and snot.

I had a hard time finding books with specific information about the nose, so it took a long time to compile all the information in this book. Most of the material about breathing comes from books about respiration, but my precise descriptions of the nose's structure were culled from medical journal articles about plastic surgery on the nose.

My final step was to speak to doctors and scientists doing nose research. These interviews ensure that the book includes the most up-to-date information about how the two sides of the nose take turns breathing and about the role noses plays in solving crimes.

—Melissa Stewart

FIND OUT MORE

BOOKS

Solway, Andrew. *The Respiratory System.* Chicago: World Book, Inc., 2007.

Taylor-Butler, Christine. *The Respiratory System.* New York: Children's Press, 2007.

Weiss, Ellen. *The Sense of Smell.* New York: Children's Press, 2008.

WEBSITES

Anatomy of the Sinuses
The diagrams on this site give you a terrific view of the sinuses.
http://www.ghorayeb.com/AnatomySinuses.html

Get Body Smart: The Nose
A complete overview of how we smell.
http://www.getbodysmart.com/ap/respiratorysystem/nose/nasalmucosa/tutorial.html

Guinness World Records
This site contains up-to-date information on some of the strangest world's records you can imagine.
http://www.guinnessworldrecords.com/default.aspx

Kids Health
This site answers just about any question about your body and keeping it healthy.
http://kidshealth.org/kid/

INDEX

Page numbers in **bold** are illustrations.

ABOUT THE AUTHOR

Melissa Stewart has written everything from board books for preschoolers to magazine articles for adults. She is the award-winning author of more than one hundred books for young readers. She serves on the board of advisors for the Society of Children's Book Writers and Illustrators and is a judge for the American Institute of Physics Children's Science Writing Award. Stewart earned a B.S. in biology from Union College and an M.A. in science journalism from New York University. She lives in Acton, Massachusetts, with her husband, Gerard. To learn more about Stewart, please visit her website: www.melissa-stewart.com.

ABOUT THE ILLUSTRATOR

Janet Hamlin has illustrated many children's books, games, newspapers, and even Harry Potter stuff. She is also a court artist. The Gross and Goofy Body is one of her all-time favorite series, and she now considers herself the factoid queen of bodily functions. She lives and draws in New York and loves it.

DATE DUE

APR 2 7 2010			
APR 1 0 REC'D			
OCT 1 4 2010			
SEP 1 4 2011			
FEB 0 2 2015			
FEB 1 5 2017			